Narcissists
On Parade

By

Bin Thaya

ISBN 9 781304 394545

Starring as Narcissists

Supporting cast

The Mother

Others in family

The Younger Sister

The Younger Brother

The Father

The father went to college. His older brother did not.

Grandiosity

The mother and father traveled the world but there was one place she wanted to visit more than any other, Ireland.

Anyone who has more than I do is a crook. Those with less are losers including my own children.

The father is enraged
because of a bad picture
taken of him!!

Every few months the father would sit the child down and show him/her how rich he was...

Narcissists laugh at inappropriate times.

You are such a loser! HA!!HA!!

Narcissistic Rage

Younger daughter earns graduate degree in liberal arts. Upon her return home she is eviscerated by the father in a narcissistic rage. Demanding she go out and get a job NOW- She goes through six, seven dead-end jobs. The mother turns a blind eye. The daughter is shattered. It will be decades before she sees this as extreme abuse and a life altering event.

The father raises triangulation to a high art-

Following the mother's death the father goes "full stop" on family traditions/get togethers.

Telling the younger daughter-

Demeaning/Bullying Behavior

Younger son and wife are killed in an accident. Choosing a casket for his son.

Choosing a headstone for his son & daughter-in-law.

Younger brother & his wife are killed in accident. They leave two boys. The deceased mother's brother adopts them. The father refuses any contact with his grandsons.

Oh, the family is uneducated. I will have nothing to do with them. I went to college. I read Reader's Digest book summaries. I am special. I have money.

Younger daughter plays late brother's music for a friend. The father enters and turns it off.

Younger daughter expresses wish she had told something to her brother before he died...the father leans in and says-

Younger daughter is a professional writer. The father says-

Near end of father's life, the younger daughter puts forth this equation:

The Older Brother

Narcissism means never having to say you're sorry.

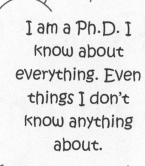

Sense of Entitlement

Older brother on younger brother's musical talent.

Seeing him, I think that could be my brother in a few years.

Younger brother & wife die in accident. Older brother writes eulogy saying their children....

Of course, I'll have nothing to do with them because their new family is uneducated. Their new dad-a laborer. I have a doctorate. I am special!!

...are an enduring legacy, a gift to us all.

And he spoke of his brother's gifts-

Never saw him play. Couldn't name one song he wrote.

The music was inside him. It was wonderful to watch his thoughts and feelings transformed through his mind and fingers into music that will be with us forever.

Lack of
Empathy

The younger sister talks of abuse by the father to her older brother.

Passive/Aggressive is a pastime of the covert narcissist.

I'll ignore her texts today. Tomorrow may reply...then again, may not.

The younger sister and older brother talk movies-

The older brother does not acknowledge gifts-

The older brother "schedules" phone calls..

Older brother writes family history.

We were rich. Hobnobbed with prominent people, whose names I have shared. We were kind to "the help." When all said & done "the perfect family."

Reacting Negatively to Criticism

The Older Sister

For her entire life the older sister did not connect with the younger sister. The older sister often ignored her. Often cut her off mid-sentence or simply walked out of a room when she spoke. Dismissed her pain & accomplishments. & Marginalized her socially.

My mind is elsewhere. Anywhere but on you!!

For her entire life the younger sister was on the receiving end of "the smirk." Often when she would speak—the older sister would react this way-

What a stupid thing to say!! UGH…

Younger brother & wife die in an accident. The older sister's estranged husband attends the funeral. The younger sister greets him.

Younger brother & wife die in an accident and leave two children. They are adopted by late wife's brother's family. The older sister joins the older brother & the father in her views.

I will have nothing to do with them because their family is not rich.

The older sister likes people with money.

We're going to be good friends!!

Exaggerating Accomplishments/ Dominating Conversations

The older sister has an exchange with a friend.

Older sister likes being the center of attention-

Younger sister asks older sister-

Why have you kept your children from me all these years?

Because you are not the kind of person, I want them to be around.

Younger sister has a nervous breakdown and older sister says—

I'm here for you now but if you pull this again, I won't be here for you.

Call the shelter hotline.

The younger sister recovered from her breakdown which was long & painful.

It was brought on by decades of narcissistic abuse.

If you experience any of the behaviors described in "Narcissists on Parade" she implores you not to walk but—

RUN, RUN, RUN for the hills!

THE END